CONTENTS

Wheels, wheels, wheels   4
Big and small wheels   6
Cog-wheels   10
Wheels in machines   12
Before wheels   14
Wheels at the building site   16
How do cranes use wheels?   20
Lots of wheels   22
Wheels at the funfair   24
The big wheel   26
Wonderful wheels!   28
Fun activities   30
Index   32

4

I WANT TO KNOW...

?

Why do we need wheels?

Helena Ramsay and Paul Humphrey

Illustrated by Stuart Trotter

First published in this edition in 2011 by
Evans Publishing Group
2A Portman Mansions
Chiltern Street
London W1U 6NR

© Evans Brothers Limited 2011

www.evansbooks.co.uk

British Library Cataloguing in Publication Data:
A CIP catalogue record for this book is available from the British Library

ISBN: 9780237544942

Planned and produced by Discovery Books
Cover designed by Rebecca Fox

For permission to reproduce copyright material the author and publishers gratefully
acknowledge the following: Art Directors Photo Library: page 24; Bruce Coleman: pages 18-18;
Mary Evans: page 9; Chris Fairclough: pages 11, 12; Image Bank: page 12; istock: cover; Robert
Harding: pages 17, 20-21, 22-23, 26.

Printed by Great Wall Printing Company in Chai Wan, Hong Kong,
August 2011, Job Number 1672.

6

Small wheels have to go round
much faster than big wheels
if they're to move along the
ground at the same speed.

8

A hundred years ago some bikes had one very big wheel and one small one.

I know, they were called penny farthings.

When you change gear
the chain moves from one
cog to another.

We can see the cog-wheels on a bike but lots of machines have wheels inside them which you can't see.

Some watches have wheels.

Before CD players, people used cassette recorders. Did you know there are wheels inside them, too?

13

14

Sometimes they used animals
to help them. Otherwise they
pushed or dragged the things
themselves. It was hard work.

Wheels make it much easier and
faster to move things around.

Here's the building site. Let's look at all the different kinds of wheels.

Big, fat wheels don't sink into the ground. The dumper truck can go over soft earth without getting stuck.

Caterpillar tracks

18

There's a bulldozer, it hasn't got any wheels.

A bulldozer has got wheels inside the caterpillar tracks. They make the tracks go round.

Did you know that wheels can be used for lifting things, too?

Do cranes have wheels?

20

It has lots of wheels so that
it can carry very heavy loads.
The weight is divided up among
all the wheels so that each one
carries only a little bit.

Bikes with only one
wheel are called unicycles. You
have to balance very carefully.

You can all have a ride on the big wheel before we go home.

That's the biggest wheel I've ever seen.

How do they make
the big wheel turn
round so fast?

There is an engine driving it round.

A motor turns the wheels on my wheelchair.

Look at me making the wheels turn on my skateboard – whoops!

28

29

Fun activities

Which is which? Match the wheels to the vehicles below. The answers are at the bottom of the page, but don't peep until you have tried yourself.

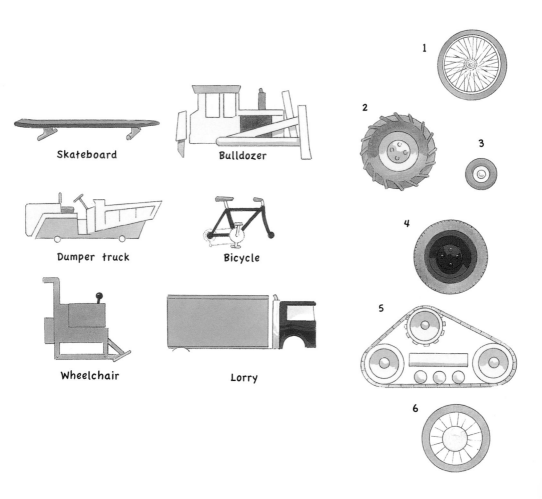

Skateboard

Bulldozer

Dumper truck

Bicycle

Wheelchair

Lorry

1

2

3

4

5

6

Answers:
1. Bicycle 2. Dumper truck 3. Skateboard 4. Lorry 5. Bulldozer 6. Wheelchair

Spot the wheels!
Over the next few days keep your eyes peeled for different types of wheels around the house and when you are on the move. What are the differences between the wheels that you see? Are they big or small? What is the function of the wheels?

Make a chart like the one below recording what you found.

What?	How many wheels?	Size?	Function
	4	Medium	To move the car

Imagine you are living in a world without wheels.
Think about how you would travel around. What do you normally do in the day that uses wheels? Would you still be able to do all of these things? Write a diary entry describing your day without wheels and how it would be different from a normal day.

Interesting websites:
This website will help you to find out more about the history and science of wheels:
http://www.historyforkids.org/scienceforkids/physics/machines/wheel.htm

Take part in some fun activities to help you learn more about how wheels work in different machines:
http://www.mikids.com/SMachinesWheels.htm

Discover what makes the wheel one of the world's greatest ever inventions.
http://www.pitara.com/magazine/features/online.asp?story=10

Index

Funfair
    big wheel 4, 25, 26, 28-29
    unicycle 24

Skateboard 27

Truck 22-23

Wheelchair 6, 27

Wheels
    carrying 22-23
    dragging 15
    lifting 20-21
    powering 26-27
    pulley 20-21
    pushing 15
    sizes 6-7, 8-9, 16-17
    speed 6-7, 15